UNDYING DEVOTION

Undying Devotion

Romantic Poetry

ARMANDO AULET

Indy Pub

CONTENTS

~ I ~

I LOVE YOU.

You are what brings order to my chaos.
Identically like Icarus,
I too was a man who had gotten burnt by the ultimate beauty of the sun.
Yet the world will proceed to revolve around it, forever,
just like I around you.
My love for you is one of the only things that I am sure of in this chaotic world,
just like I am sure that the sun will rise tomorrow.

I LOVE WHEN YOU CRY

I love when you cry,
it makes me feel relieved.
That may sound sick in many, many ways,
and I apologize for it.
Though, I need you to understand, my relief is never from your saddened tears.
It's simply because you're alive enough to cry those tears.
Alive enough to cry,
alive enough to sob,
no matter how broken you are, you're breathing.
Though I'm a selfish, very selfish man,
as long as your heart is still beating,
pounding against your rib-cage as if trying to kill you.
As long as you are alive, I am too.

YOU HOLD BEAUTY LIKE NO OTHER

Before I met you I had thought the moon was the most beautiful thing to ever exist.

Lord, only the heavens and the earth know how wrong I was.

My dear, even the most perfect of angels turn their heads in awe,

they envy the look in my eyes when they meet you.

Once my eyes lay upon you, they can't help but glow,

basking in your ultimate perfection.

You hold beauty like no other,

and you hold me in a captive embrace, entranced by such delicacy.

I FELL IN LOVE WITH YOU

I didn't fall in love with you because I had to.
You'd be so, so wrong.
My dear, I fell in love with you because when I wake up every single morning,
the first thought that floods my empty mind is you.
You captivate my heart, mind, and my entire being.
Till I take my final breath.
When that time comes, It will be a breath of satisfaction,
knowing my soul will forever be intertwined with yours,
and the undying love between us.
For my soul is yours, and will always be attracted to you.

I BELONG TO YOU

Your heart has touched mine,
it was then that our souls, and our worlds, had collided.
At that instant, my heart was so full of you,
it became yours in its entirety.
You had gained full possession of it, of me.
I belong to you.

UNEXPLAINABLE CONNECTION

We have a connection that can't quite be explained.
A connection that can't be duplicated.
The relationship between the moon and the stars,
the relationship between the galaxies and the universe,
are nothing compared to us.
No matter how beautiful they display themselves,
no matter how hard they may try,
they can't do it,
they can never do it.
They are nothing like us,
they can never be us.

BEAUTY LIES WITHIN THE EYES OF THE BEHOLDER

They say beauty lies within the eyes of the beholder, but the way you manage to sway me with such an embrace, even the blind has the opportunity to experience your strong and radiating beauty.

My love, every step you take in this world,

every step you take in this universe,

Angels themselves are left questioning their own perfection.

They look at you and they can't help but bask in your glory,

having complete envy over the fact that the beings who are symbols of perfection, are no longer perfect, compared to you.

DROWNING AND BURNING

I drown in the deep depths that is your eyes,
yet you turn my heart into a fiery inferno.
filling my lungs with smoke and water, causing me to choke on your beauty.

THE HEAVENS

If I were to ever reach up to the heavens and bathe in the light of those big pearly gates,

I wouldn't help but chuckle,

laughing at their lousy attempt of perfection and beauty.

I'll look around, examining, analyzing.

Coming to the conclusion that, the place where everything is supposed to be perfect, couldn't replicate your flawlessness.

BEAUTIFUL RADIANCE

There is nothing more artistic,

nothing more elegant and beautiful than the love between us.

Even the relationship between the moon and the stars cannot out-shine your beautiful radiance.

Even the sun doesn't stand a chance against you.

There is no winning.

There is no competition.

There is only you.

FRAGMENTS FROM OUR STARS

We are all made out of fragments from our beautiful stars.

Yet, you still shine brighter than everyone and anyone else, how unfair.

Guess the heavens do have favorites.

SOFT HANDS

I love you because you have touched my heart ever so softly.

Treating it with the utmost care while the world had treated it with so much cruelty.

FOREVER

I'll lay with you till the sun no longer burns and the moon is turned into dust.

I'll love you till the clock runs out of time and the world ends.

I'll be with you till my soul finds you again in another life, and till our worlds collide once more.

THIS LIFETIME

My soul has lived a thousand lifetimes.

Yet this lifetime, with you, is the only lifetime ever worth remembering, and the only lifetime ever worth living again.

PEACE OF MIND

You have given me something I have never experienced with anyone before, something I didn't think was realistically possible.

Peace, and peace of mind.

It felt like the silence after a tragedy.

The calmness after the rain.

Standing in the chaos of what once was, but is no longer.

Finally being open.

Finally being free.

MOON, STARS, SUN, EARTH

Everyday I will look at you with eyes full of adoration and love as if you were the very person who created the moon and the stars.

As if you were the very person who created the sun and earth.

As if you were the very person who created all that is beautiful.

ONE DAY

One day i'm going to leave this earth.

One day my soul will need to find a new vessel, and in that vessel, whoever they may possibly be, I will find you.

No grave can take me from you.

I will always come back to you, in every lifetime.

And when there is no earth, and when there are no more vessels left to inhabit, I hope we can be stardust together.

JUST ETERNITY

I will always find you.

I'm meant to.

When there are no more lives left to live, and when all there is is a void of darkness, I hope we make our own heaven.

Only for us.

No gods, no graves, no tears.

Just eternity.

NOTHINGNESS

When all falls quiet in the universe,
I hope those very last moments before nothingness are spent in the stars with you.

EVERY FORM I TAKE

Oh how I hope to be beside you in every form I take.

Human, animal, plant, god, star, I want it all to be with you.

It'll all be worth it, if I were to spend it with you.

I WANT IT ALL WITH YOU

I want to spend every lifetime with you, my love.

Staying up late, laughing, kissing, crying, I want it all with you.

All until we become a nebula that humans will gaze at in awe.

Until time bends and the sky falls upon us.

A LOVE WITHIN GRACE

One day people will look up at the stars,
and we'll be sitting on moonbeams, and dancing on stars.
We'll be jumping around, and skipping on constellations.
A love upon space.
A love within grace.

I WILL LOVE YOU UNTIL

I will love you until I burn up from the inside out.

I will love you until I take my place within the stars.

I will love you until the universe collapses in on itself.

I will love you with every fiber of my being, with every life I have ever lived before this one.

NO ONE ELSE

Love never manifests itself the same way twice.

There is no one who will ever live that I would rather watch the end of time with.

No matter the kind of love.

I would want no one else to be star dust with me.

I would want no one else to spend my last moments with.

IT ALWAYS LEADS BACK TO US

If you never find me, I'll always find you.

In every lifetime.

In every universe.

Even if you don't remember me, even if you want me gone.

I will always reappear.

At the end of the day it leads back to you, It always does.

It always leads back to us.

TYPES OF LOVE

There are always at least three types of love people can endure.

People who claim to love.

People who claim to kill.

Lastly, people who claim they are willing to die.

But I am like no other man, I love you beyond that.

My love, I love you like no other, so I will live for you, in this god forsaken world.

All for you.

Only for you.

KNOWING, FEELING

I tell you that I love you many, many times per day, so you never, ever forget.

Though, my love, I show you that I love you so you can feel it, instead of simply knowing it because you hear it.

HAVING YOU

Having you is like having my own personal star.
The things that shine bright in the night skies.
The things that scientists take years to understand.
No matter what anybody does, they will never have you the way I have you.
They will never quite understand you the way I do.

DEEPEST SECRETS, DEEPEST DESIRES

You can tell me your darkest past and your deepest secrets.

You can tell me your darkest nightmares and your deepest desires.

I will always look at you with love and adoration within my eyes, I will always look at you as if you can do no wrong.

I will always look at you as if you are the sun, no matter how much darkness you may carry within.

IF NOT

Our souls are far too tangled into one another's to ever be separated again.

To ever be apart.

I'll always be with you, every step of the way.

If not in person, then always in spirit.

If not in person, then always within your heart.

UNEXPECTED

I find it crazy that you were the most unexpected person, in the most unexpected time.

Even with this, my soul had felt as if it was expecting you for years.

My heart felt as if it had been yearning for yours.

It felt such a familiarity with you.

Now that we are together, both my heart, and my soul, feel complete.

I CAN PROMISE YOU

I am incapable of protecting your heart from others, I have no such power to do so.

Even with this, I can promise you, I am capable of making sure you never have to go through any heartache alone.

YOU OVER ME

You hold so much power over me.

You smile a smile that has never made me smile more than ever before.

Your simple actions have such an effect on me.

Such a power over me.

CAPTIVATED

The sun, moon, and stars can try their absolute best to out-shine you.

Trying so hard to persuade me to go and gaze into their enchanting glance, to have me bathe in their light.

But I could never, nothing can pull my eyes away from you, for you have captivated me in your very own light.

LOVING ME, LOVING YOU

You have made me comfortable in loving myself, which has caused me to love you even more than ever.

You had done something for me that I couldn't do for myself.

Loving me, helps me love you.

OBLIVIOUS

My love, what a mighty plot twist you were.

For so long, we were right in front of each other, oblivious to what the world had in store for us.

It had been so clear, yet we were so blind.

LIVE, LAUGH, LOVE

Your smile stole my heart, and your eyes had given me life.

Your laugh sends me among the clouds, and I want nothing more than to spend forever in this comfy, and blissful state with you.

WISHES

Even when the world had been against us, I put my hand out to you.

Even with the chaos around us, you so bravely took it,
going against all wishes, but granting our own.

IF YOU WERE NO MORE

The agonizing feeling that I would have to endure if I were to continue living in a world where you were no more.

I'd look for you in the stars, but you'd be all alone, you're without me.

I'd reach up, but cannot touch you.

Dream of you, but cannot see you.

Keep your clothes, but cannot smell you.

Kiss your photos, but cannot taste you.

Call your phone, but will never hear you.

WORTH LIVING

There is no other like you, you are truly one of a kind.
With such deep desire,
I desire you to be the light at the end of the tunnel,
for there is no after life worth living, without your radiance.
I was blinded the moment I had laid my eyes upon you.
Though my sight had been taken away from me, grief wasn't the result,
for in that instance, I had truly gazed upon ultimate perfection.
If it was a sin to stare into your eyes,
to witness such ecstasy,
no god could save me from the inevitable consequences.
I would be condemned to eternal agony as long as my soul exists.
No being would ever want such a thing, but I'd do it again, and again,
just to experience you.

SAY, DO, WHO YOU ARE

You hold such a beauty that is not only in looks,
but it is in what you say,
what you do,
and who you are.
You have a beauty that will never falter.
A beauty that will never die.

EVERYTHING BECAME ABOUT YOU

It's astounding how the moment we collided,
the moment I fell,
everything became about you.
Books, music, TV, I always look for you in them.
Someone or something that resembles you.
Someone or something that makes me think of you.
Perhaps someone or something I think you'd simply like.
I look for you everywhere.
I look for you in everything.

I WILL SPEAK

I can speak about you till the world ends.
I can talk and talk till my lungs give out and I am no more.
I will speak to the gods and to the goddesses about you,
I will speak to the moon and the stars about you,
I will speak to the sun and the planets about you.
I will preach your beauty and perfection till the universe forcefully takes my voice away.
Even then, I will write for you.
Page after page, a never ending love.

NO GRAVE NOR GOD

No grave nor god can hold my body.

I will tear my flesh right off of my bones just to get back into your arms.

I will tear my eyes out of their sockets if it meant I'll get to see you in the after life too.

I'd do anything if it means I get to be with you and experience you,

in this life, and the next.

TO MY POEMS

Oh how I love you so,
writing for you, reading for you.
You are my muse,
my inspiration,
my cause.
I may be the writer, but you'll always be the theme to my romantic poems;
to my poems of love,
to my poems of beauty,
to my poems of perfection.
It'll always be you.

NO MATTER HOW HARD

When I pass on, I want someone to find my writings,
to find my projects, to find my poems, and be baffled that this kind of love was ever achievable.
Although, I don't think anyone will,
no matter how hard I try,
no matter how hard anyone tries,
It'll never be possible to describe both the connection, and love between us.

I CAN NEVER STOP

People can read my words,

understand what I am trying to convey,

but they will never, ever truly understand the feeling and passion that lies behind them.

They will never, ever understand the true love and devotion I have within me; but oh I can never stop.

I can never stop writing for you.

I can never stop trying to display my undying devotion to you.

I'll run out of paper long before I'll ever run out of the will to write for you.

ALL OF ME

I am such a hopeless romantic for you, my love.
I'll do anything you desire, anything you need.
I'll give you food right off my plate if I have to.
I'll give you the shirt right off of my back if I have to.
Oh I'll even let you take absolutely anything you want from me.
Ill give it all to you, all of my possessions,
all of me.

JUST SOME PERSON

You were never just some person to me.
Oh how I lay my head on my pillow,
closing my eyes only to be greeted by you.
You see, even my subconscious knew you weren't just some person.
The universe had brought us together,
the universe has shown me you were never just some person,
and oh how thankful I am that it did.

FIND ANOTHER

With all of the lives you will live, I am confident to say you will never find another quite like me.

You'll never find another who loves and cherishes you the way I do.

You'll never find another who is so devoted and loyal to you the way I am.

Oh my love, we fit perfectly, like pieces in a puzzle, if you go seek another, the two of you will never be compatible.

Both of you will never fit together.

Oh but when you are with me, we could never fit more perfectly.

~ II ~

I LOVE WHO YOU WERE.

I'm glad you're gone,
but at times I do still miss you.
I miss the person I first met,
the person who actually cared about me.
The person I thought you truly were.

EVENTUALLY

Eventually, you learn to stop trying to force someone who hurts you, to treat you better.

Eventually, you realize you should treat yourself better, by walking away instead.

YOU CAN

You can love someone and proceed to acknowledge that they are not good for you.

You can also miss someone and proceed to let them go.

WANT, NEED

One of the hardest things to do,
is to leave what you know you want,
for something you know you need.

DEAD TO ME

Having to witness someone you had grown so attached to,
someone you had once bonded with,
vanish.
It's like mourning the death of someone who didn't die,
but had become dead to you.

DEADLY, DESIRED

Love is the most deadliest thing, yet the most desired.

Getting our hearts broken, just to go and find another that may do the exact same thing.

Confining in a person who swears they will do you no wrong.

While the last person had promised you that exact same thing.

WONDERING

You had left me wondering if you truly ever loved me.

Left me wondering if I just simply loved you enough that I had been able to pretend that you actually loved me just as much as I loved you.

COMPLEXITY

Love is an extremely complex thing.

If you love someone too much, they may just fall in love with the love you have for them,

they wont fall in love with you.

And if you don't love someone enough, they will seek another that will love them more than you ever could.

CHARACTERS

I was nothing but a mere side character in your book, the comedic relief.

While I had written story after story for you; you were the love interest, the hero,

someone important, the way you were important to me.

I guess I was just a joke to you.

CUPID IS CRUEL

Cupid is a cruel, vile man.

He had me fall in love with someone who had never fallen in love with me in the first place.

It hurt worse than Cupid's piercing arrows penetrating my skin.

It hurt worse than the arrows penetrating through my heart.

DECEPTION

As I am surrounded by the shards of my fragmented heart.

I finally realized that the love I had held onto so, so tightly, was merely a cruel deception.

A deception that tore my soul apart with its betrayal.

I WANTED NOTHING MORE

I watched as you walked away, fading into the distance.

Even though tragedy had corrupted our harmony, I wanted nothing more than to fade away with you.

INNOCENT, GUILTY

I had done everything in my power to preach your innocence, to preach that you weren't as bad of a person that it may have seemed.

While I did that, you did everything in your power to preach that I was the one who was guilty.

That I was the one who was at fault.

NEVER, EVER

I had thought that you were finally showing me what love was actually like,

what love should be.

You were actually showing me a lesson on what love should never, ever be.

MYSELF

My heart has darkened, but my eyes have opened.
I'll better my own heart,
I'll wipe my own tears.
Though I had you, all I ever really had was myself.

HAPPENED TO DO IT WRONG

I wish you know how it completely destroyed me when we had parted ways.

I like to think we would have worked,
we just happened to do it wrong.

MAYBE IN ANOTHER LIFETIME

Maybe in another lifetime,
maybe in another universe,
we would get along.
Maybe in another lifetime,
maybe in another universe,
the bond we had would never be broken.
Maybe in another lifetime,
maybe in another universe,
we were mean't to be.

APOLOGY

I deserve the biggest and most heartfelt apology,
from both myself, and from you.
You put me through hell,
while I let you experience heaven.

YOU REALIZE

One day I hope you wake up and realize that I was worth treating right,

that I was indeed worth fighting for.

I hope you realize that you'll never be worth another chance,

and that I will indeed not be fighting for you.

I HATE MYSELF

I hate myself for the fact that I don't hate *you.*
For the fact I can't hate you.
I hate myself for the fact I only hate you for what you *did.*

DELETE

I can delete everything that had anything to do with you,
your social media,
your number,
I can delete every trace that you had ever existed in my life.
That was the easy part.
Even after all of that, I can't delete the memories of you,
the memories of us.
I can't delete the things that seemed to actually matter to me.
The things that seemed to actually eat me alive.
That was the excruciating part.

WHY WOULD YOU

I need to get rid of the false hope that you will ever change.

Why would you change now, when you didn't change then?

Why would you change now, when you didn't change when I begged you?

Why would you change now, when you didn't change when I cried to you?

Why would you change now, when I had given you every chance in the world?

You had every opportunity,

You're the one who didn't take it.

So why should I keep a false hope when it is exactly that, *false.*

MY FAULT

I'm not all to blame.

Why would it be my fault that I got hurt for believing the promises you promised to keep?

TIME PERIOD

I miss the time period where I actually mean't something to you.

The time period where I was actually what you wanted.

Where I was actually what you desired.

SETTLING IN

I hated waking up the next morning and really realizing that the true reality was that everything was final.

That there was nothing I could ever do.

That there was nothing I could ever say.

Getting that dreaded feeling as though your heart is physically breaking in your chest.

Then having to go about your day as if your life had not just been altered merely hours prior.

Life really does go on.

No matter what.

WE ARE NOT THE SAME

I had destroyed myself just so you had comfort and security.

You destroyed me just so you had entertainment and control.

We are not the same.

GUT WRENCHING

I have always hated that deep, gut wrenching feeling you gave me.

The fear of starting an argument,

the fear of you getting in your feelings,

the fear of you getting aggressive,

but most of all, I hated the gut wrenching feeling of not knowing what to do with you,

of not knowing what to do with myself.

CARE

The audacity you had to tell me that I had never cared about you.

About us.

When in all actuality, all I ever did was care too much.

EMBARRASSED

Sometimes I'm embarrassed to miss you,
after everything you had done to me.
Sometimes I'm embarrassed to love you,
after everything you had said to me.

OIL/WATER

No matter how much they try,
oil and water can never mix.
Even if they appear to combine for just a singular moment,
they were destined to separate since the start.

MAYBE THAT'S WHY

I miss the laughs and the good times we had,
and maybe that's why I stayed for so long.
I was fighting for the good and comforting memories that had lived on in my head.
The memories I had wished to feel again.
The memories I had wished to experience again.

IT'S DIFFICULT TO FORGET

It's difficult.

It's difficult to forget someone who had given you so much to remember,

whether it be good, or bad.

It's difficult to forget the good memories since all they do is remind you that this wasn't the way it was supposed to end.

It's difficult to forget the bad memories since all they do is remind you that everything that was once good, had gone sour,

had gone bitter, distasteful.

It's a reminder that everything wasn't always this way.

SEA OF FACES'

At least I had shown the truth of my darkness.

Yet, you, were you always like this?

Or did I taint yet another thing of beauty I just wanted to hold so close?

As I looked back, I had come to the realization that I never held the memory of you close enough.

You faded into the sea of faces', ones I can never see again.

The ones I can never forget about.

THE STAGES OF GRIEF

Grief doesn't go away.
In fact, sometimes it may just grow.
But we grow as people,
and we grow to learn how to accept it.
How to make it hurt less.

LOVE/LUST

They can tell you that they love you all they want.

But there is a difference between knowing love, and feeling love.

Knowing the difference between love, and lust.

STUPID PROMISES

I feel stupid for believing that they meant forever when forever is not even forever to them.

NEVER SAW YOU AGAIN

It sucks when you expect to see someone again but you never do.

You never get an official goodbye,
you never get to hold them one last time,
you never get to hold them just a little tighter.

DID YOU MEAN THEM?

Sometimes I lay,
just thinking,
pondering,
If you ever truly meant the loving things you had said to me,
the same way you meant the vile ones.

WE DIDN'T DESERVE

It's crazy that I loved you so much that even when you did me wrong,
when you treated me in ways I never deserved,
I treated you in ways you didn't deserve.

BLAME, HATE

Ill never, ever blame you for not loving me.

But I sure as hell will hate you for pretending that you did.

PREMEDITATED

It's disturbing how comfortable and nonchalant you were after hurting me.

It's as if you meant to,
wanted to,
planned to.

It's as if I was just some game to you.

BETTER, TOGETHER

What if us having to part ways was meant to be?
Only for us to better ourselves.
I just wish we would have gotten better, together.

FALSE HOPE

I spent months trying to get over you,
only for you to appear in my dreams.
It makes me think that your finally thinking of me,
it makes me think that atleast we work out in some other universe.

CAUSE AND EFFECT

It's weird how you hated when I'd confront you because the things I say may be mean or insulting,

but you never hated the fact that what I was saying was true.

If you hated it so much, why would you continue to act that way to the point it continues to drive me to confront you?

I DESERVE

I deserved a better life.
I deserved a better relationship.
Most of all, I deserved a better goodbye.
I deserved a better apology.

I HOPE

I hope I run through your head and you genuinely wonder how you were able to just let me go.

How you were able to ever seek another.

How you were able to ever do me wrong.

GO AHEAD AND LEAVE

You can go look for anyone and anything you want.

But you'll realize that I gave you a type of love that youll never experience again.

A love you didnt deserve.

IF YOU WANTED TO, YOU WOULD

I craved your love and desire,
your appreciation and affection.
I wanted you to show that you loved and cared for me the way you once did.
I sit and stare at you, pondering on what I could possibly do,
but I remember,
I did everything in my power.
If you really wanted to show me that you felt any love towards me,
you would.

WHY SHOULD I?

Why should I apologize for being so broken?
Why should I apologize for being so cruel?
Why should I apologize for being the person you pushed me to be?
Why should I apologize for treating you the way you treated me?

THE END

No matter how much I may love you,
No matter how much I may miss you,
I'd rather stab myself in the chest before ever giving you the chance to stab me in the back.
I'll never let you be the end of me.
I'll be the end of you.
The end of us.

Armando Aulet was born in the year 2006, in Worcester, Massachusetts. Growing up, he had a fascination for drawing, this fascination later grew into him writing his own short stories, stories that later transformed themselves into poems. Armando, who now studies carpentry, developed a passion for writing poetry as a method of showing deep emotion that is unable to be displayed any other way. Undying Devotion is Mr. Aulet's first book.

Milton Keynes UK
Ingram Content Group UK Ltd.
UKHW020630200524
442968UK00001B/58